Images of Modern America

LGBTQ LAS VEGAS

Images of Modern America

LGBTQ LAS VEGAS

Dennis McBride

ARCADIA
PUBLISHING

Published by Arcadia Publishing
Charleston, South Carolina

Printed in the United States of America

Library of Congress Control Number: 2017936682

For all general information, please contact Arcadia Publishing:
Telephone 843-853-2070
Fax 843-853-0044
E-mail sales@arcadiapublishing.com
For customer service and orders:
Toll-Free 1-888-313-2665

Visit us on the Internet at www.arcadiapublishing.com

This book is for the Nevada LGBTQ community whose fortitude, perseverance, and mutual support have made our state one of the most progressive in the nation in support of queer equality.

CONTENTS

ACKNOWLEDGMENTS

The opportunity for me to produce this book was serendipitous. I had been working for more than 40 years researching and writing *Out of the Neon Closet: Queer Community in the Silver State*, a comprehensive history of Nevada's LGBTQ community, and was wrapping up the final draft when I had a telephone call from Raul Mangubat, manager of Las Vegas' LGBTQ bookstore, Get Booked. Arcadia Publishing was looking for someone who could produce a pictorial history of the Las Vegas queer community for its Images of Modern America series. Raul suggested me, and I was eager for the opportunity. I was limited in *Neon Closet* to just 40 images. With thousands to choose from, it was difficult to pick just 40 photographs to illustrate a history that spans more than 150 years. There were remarkable images from the queer community I regretted might never be seen, but Arcadia offered a chance to share them. I would like to thank Raul for recommending me for this project and Arcadia Publishing for the opportunity.

I would also like to thank those dozens of LGBTQ individuals and organizations whose generosity and cooperation during the last four decades helped me build the LGBTQ archive, now housed in the Special Collections Division of the University of Nevada, Las Vegas' Lied Library (UNLV Libraries Special Collections & Archives) and curated by Su Kim Chung. This is the largest such archive in the Mountain West, which I hope will be the source eventually for more books, papers, and studies. While there are too many to thank by name here, I have been able to make my and the community's gratitude clear through their appearance in the images of *LGBTQ Las Vegas*.

INTRODUCTION

LGBTQ Las Vegas details the history and culture of Las Vegas' queer community. While Nevada has long promoted itself as philosophically libertarian, it has actually been socially and politically conservative. The future state's territorial legislature in 1861 adopted English common law, which included the "infamous crime against nature." Nevada used its sodomy law to intimidate and prosecute gay men until it was repealed in 1993 by the state legislature. Until then, Nevada's queer citizens were discouraged from establishing community and fighting for the same rights, privileges, and responsibilities enjoyed by Nevada's straight citizens.

Las Vegas, however, is an anomaly with a richly varied history. It has served as a watering stop for westward explorers; a short-lived Mormon outpost; a farming and mining settlement; a division point on the San Pedro, Los Angeles & Salt Lake Railroad; and a marriage and divorce capital. Las Vegas sailed through the Great Depression on the Hoover Dam project and benefited from such government largesse as Nellis Air Force Base and the Nevada Test Site in the 1940s and 1950s. Las Vegas has always gone its own way and is today a destination resort known across the world for its extravagant gaming palaces, sumptuous entertainment, and world-class dining. With nearly 2.5 million people, Greater Las Vegas houses more than 70 percent of Nevadans and is home to the state's most diverse population. Among these are LGBTQ advocates from throughout the nation who have enriched Las Vegas' queer community with their experience and expertise. Las Vegas has become a blue island in a red sea and is today among the most progressive and hospitable US cities in welcoming LGBTQ citizens and visitors.

LGBTQ Las Vegas traces the development of Las Vegas' queer community through four historic phases. "Building Community" details the struggle to establish the foundation of shared identity, experience, and values necessary to begin fighting for recognition and equality. "Establishing Politics" describes the community's efforts to establish the organizations and traditions it needed to enter the state's political conversation. "Fighting for Life and Equality" follows the community's direct action to achieve queer-friendly legislation despite the AIDS epidemic of the 1980s and 1990s and in the face of fierce antigay backlash from Nevada's conservative opposition. The last chapter, "The Queering of Las Vegas," details the queer community's success in at last becoming a valued and integral part of the richly diverse life of Las Vegas.

One

BUILDING COMMUNITY

While Las Vegas has long epitomized an "anything goes" morality, that freewheeling attitude for nearly 150 years did not include the city's queer community. Nevada's LGBTQ citizens, like their brothers and sisters throughout the United States, were targeted: politicians legislated against them, religionists damned them, and law enforcement arrested them. In 1861, three years before Nevada gained statehood, the Nevada Territory's legislative assembly adopted English common law, including the "infamous crime against nature," commonly known as the sodomy law. Anyone charged with sodomy faced a term in the territorial prison of five years to life. Until it was repealed in 1993, what became known as Nevada Revised Statute 201.190 was used to suppress, blackmail, and persecute queer men in Nevada.

Nevertheless, the community persevered and struggled to establish itself. Before the community could develop the political consciousness it needed to fight for its rights, it developed a social consciousness in such venues as bars, baths, and bookstores. While these venues traditionally were sexual hunting grounds, they also provided opportunities for LGBTQ people to connect with one another, share joy and grievance, establish a common identity, and celebrate queer traditions such as Gay Pride and National Coming Out Day.

While bars, baths, and bookstores provided early platforms for the development of queer community, these places were segregated from the straight world. It was the community of female impersonators who built the bridge. While straight Nevadans of the mid-20th century might not be caught dead in a gay bar, they paid money to be entertained by gay men dressed as women. While female impersonators might have inspired stereotypical perceptions of gay men, it was nonetheless these entertainers who often provided straight people their first glimpse of gay community. With their gay lives and their straight audiences, female impersonators brought both worlds together.

In 1911, Ben Etchegon accused Reno, Nevada, prizefighter John Carey of forcing him to have sex. Carey got five years in prison. During appeal, it was revealed that Etchegon had seduced Carey. Etchegon fled Reno before a second trial, and the Nevada Supreme Court overturned Carey's conviction, noting how easy it was to bring such a charge and how difficult to defend against it. (Courtesy of Nevada State Archives.)

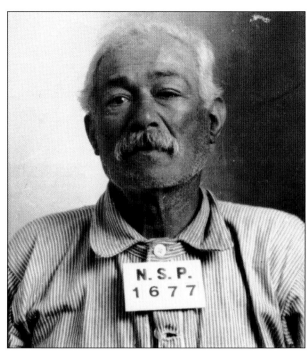

"Coyote Frank" Benites was convicted of sodomy for oral sex in 1914. Against arguments that Nevada's sodomy law pertained only to anal sex—the "infamous crime against nature"—Nevada Supreme Court justice Patrick McCarran broadened the definition of sodomy in Nevada to include any kind of sex between men—consensual or not, public or private—illegal and punishable with a prison term. (Both, courtesy of Nevada State Archives.)

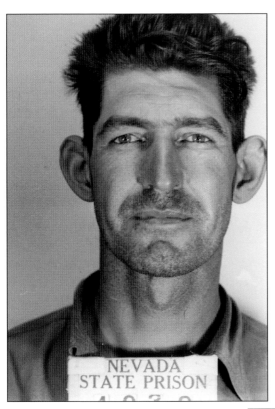

Thomas Owens, a Methodist minister from McGill, Nevada, jailed for sodomy in 1939, struggled to understand his sexual orientation in a jailhouse journal. Owens pleaded for society "to properly teach sex as it should be taught." (Courtesy of Nevada State Archives.)

On November 26, 1944, twenty-four-year-old LaDell McKay robbed and murdered Robert Flindt on Reno's East Fourth Street, was convicted of first-degree murder, and was sentenced to death. Claiming "gay panic," McKay said Flindt made a pass at him and, blind with anger, he beat Flindt to death. Robbery was only an afterthought. Both the Nevada and US Supreme Courts turned down McKay's appeals. (Courtesy of Nevada State Archives.)

Wealth, influence, and political power did not matter if a man were outed—his life was destroyed. Nevada lieutenant governor Fred Alward, on the verge of a successful run for governor in 1938, was blackmailed by a political rival, lost both his political and professional careers, and left Nevada soon after. (Author's collection.)

When Nevada Supreme Court chief justice Frank McNamee was beaten senseless in 1965 by Philipe Denning, a young man he picked up for sex at Lake Tahoe, the case was covered up and never went to public trial in order to prevent embarrassing the state. McNamee died without justice in 1968, and Denning was paroled four months later. (Author's collection.)

Gay bars provided sanctuary for the queer community before Stonewall. Maxine's opened about 1950 on the eastern outskirts of Las Vegas. A raucous bar with donkey baseball games staged in the surrounding desert, it was often isolated by flash floods during monsoon season. Bartender Billie Sweet is shown here at Maxine's in 1963, while two women play pool in the 1970s. Maxine's closed in January 1989. (Both, author's collection.)

One of Las Vegas' most famous bars was Le Café, opened by Marge Jacques on January 16, 1970, on Paradise Road and Tropicana Avenue. The bar was a popular hangout for such Las Vegas celebrities as Liberace, Joan Rivers, Shirley MacLaine, Bobbie Gentry, and Debbie Reynolds. As the LGBTQ community grew, Le Café became its de facto community center. (Above, author's collection; right, courtesy of *Panorama* magazine, February 2, 1970.)

LE CAFE: Anyone for a Scotch Sour? Owner Marge displays her pouring talent for us at this popular new night spot.

On August 24, 1978, Le Café was torched. Marge Jacques is shown here the morning after the fire counting both her and the community's losses. (Author's collection.)

Until 1972, when the Red Barn became all gay, all the time, the bar was straight by day but gay after the "pink hour" of midnight. Shown here on August 24, 1984, the Red Barn stood on Tropicana Avenue near Maryland Parkway. After closing permanently on March 31, 1988, the abandoned bar burned to the ground on September 11 that year. (Above, author's collection; below, courtesy of *Panorama* magazine, February 26, 1971.)

FEMALE IMPERSONATORS Lee J. Sommers and Rick Lane "The Fabulous Fakes" flank Flip and Dave Booth at the RED BARN and are served by Bunny "Sam" West who is obviously not a fake.

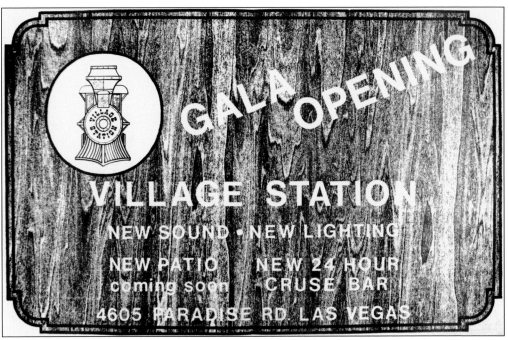

Las Vegas queer bars were often raided and harassed by local authorities. The Village Station on Paradise Road was closed in November 1980 after a sting operation conducted by the Las Vegas Metropolitan Police Department found men hugging and kissing in "blatant physical contact." The bar reopened on April 1, 1981, as Gipsy. (Above, courtesy of *Action* magazine, July 1980; below, courtesy of *Vegas Gay Times*, December 1980.)

Page 4   December, 1980   Vegas Gay Times

COUNTY CLOSES DISCO
Secret Police Surveillance Revealed

by Alan Shawn

LAS VEGAS—Undercover Metro police officers spent a total of five hours in an unmarked van videotaping patrons of the Village Station disco on two different occasions, it was revealed November 26. A half-hour edited version of the film, shown to the Clark County Commission during a hearing on the bar's liquor license application, appeared later that evening as part of several local television stations' news coverage. Testimony was also taken under oath

The major charges made at the hearing were of alleged drug dealing and usage. One person was identified by Holland as having been seen earlier behind the bar; later an individual said to be the same person was shown dealing drugs (Manager Jacques later denied under oath that they were one and the same person). Charges of alleged drug use and sales at the disco almost resulted in its being closed as far back as early 1979, when Wayne Thorberg was promoting it under the name "Studio 4."

'Riot' feared

Commissioner David Canter demanded to know several times during the tape why no arrests for drug dealing were made. Det. Holland at first stated that only four officers were on the scene and "We did not want to cause a riot." Pressed for a more plausi-

fact, all seven of them are male"), frequently referred to some of the patrons' "skimpy costumes," and seemed baffled by what he referred to as a continual "parading around the establishment...This seems to be a common practice." Manager Jacques later explained that, it being the night of the Halloween contest, patrons were filing around the building to the rear entrance to the stage (in order to avoid the dense crowd inside).

With one exception, consisting of fondling by two irresponsible patrons, the "blatent physical contact" referred to continually by the Metro narrator consisted of hugging and kissing.

Petition investigated

Roland Gregg, a private investigator, was hired by the Village Station to investigate a petition signed by area residents and submitted to the Commissioners last month. The petition alleged excessive sound levels, illegal drug usage,

The Gipsy nightclub on Paradise Road and Naples Drive is shown here on September 6, 1996. (Author's collection.)

Three pioneer Las Vegas bar owners are here honored at an "Old Timers" recognition event at the Backdoor Lounge on May 24, 1998. Pictured from left to right are Marge Jacques of Le Café (1970) and Village Station/Gipsy (1980–1981), Ralph Vandersnick of Snick's Place (1976), and Maxine Perron of Maxine's (around 1950). (Courtesy of Rob Schlegel.)

Las Vegas bathhouses were places where gay men could make anonymous sexual connections. Vegas Club Baths, opened in May 1971 as the Sir Gay Men's Spa at 1413 South Main Street, advertised private rooms, steam rooms, a movie room, and offered a "2 people for the price of 1" deal on Mondays. This advertisement from the late 1970s features a saguaro cactus whose metaphorical significance is obvious. (Author's collection.)

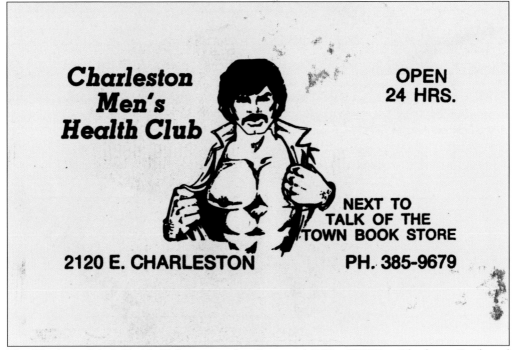

The Charleston Men's Health Club was open briefly around 1980 at 2120 East Charleston Boulevard in the Crestwood Shopping Center, where there were several porno theater/bookstores, many of which catered to gay men. (Courtesy of *Action* magazine, July 1980.)

The Camp David bathhouse opened on January 20, 1980, at 2631 Highland Drive. Even though staff gave out free condoms and safe-sex literature early in the AIDS epidemic, Las Vegas authorities frequently raided and harassed the place. Camp David closed in June 1986. The bathhouse is shown here on August 24, 1984. (Author's collection.)

On September 9, 1996, the Apollo Spa and Health Club was opened in Commercial Center on Sahara Avenue by German expatriate Torsten Reineck. When Andrew Cunanan shot Gianni Versace to death in Miami on July 15, 1997, authorities in Las Vegas connected Reineck to the crime. Pictured here are the entrance and hot pool of the Apollo on September 9, 1996. (Both, author's collection.)

Gay pornography was easily available in the adult bookstore/theaters, which began opening in Las Vegas in the 1960s–1970s. Among the first of these was the Flick, which opened at 719 East Fremont Street on November 8, 1969, with Andy Warhol's *I, A Man*. Manager John Turnquist here welcomes the Flick's first patrons. (Courtesy of *Panorama* magazine, December 12, 1969.)

FLICK THEATRE: Chuck Abel dispenses a ticket to Mark Keeling at the Flick. The first Experimental Art Theatre in Las Vegas.

The Flick advertised itself as Las Vegas' first "Experimental Art Theatre." By 1977, the Flick was all gay, with such features as *Wonderful World of Guys* and *Boys in the Round*. (Courtesy of *Panorama* magazine, January 30, 1970.)

The Crestwood Shopping Center at Eastern Avenue and Charleston Boulevard in 1973 was renamed the Adult Center for its collection of pornographic businesses. The Talk of the Town Bookstore and movie arcade, opened in September 1970, was the first adult business in Las Vegas to openly advertise its gay merchandise in the commercial press. Talk of the Town is shown here on August 24, 1984. (Author's collection.)

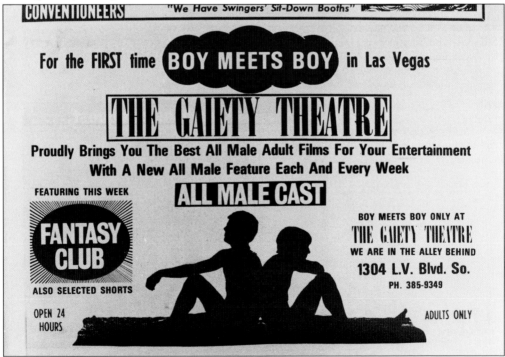

In September 1972, the former Phil's Strip Theatre, located in an alley behind 1304 Las Vegas Boulevard South, became the Gaiety Theatre and was the first such all-gay venue in town. (Courtesy of *Panorama* magazine, September 29, 1972.)

R&R Assordid Sundries was Las Vegas' first gay bookstore without a sexual focus. Opening on February 14, 1984, it provided meeting space and a wide selection of queer political literature. The Las Vegas community was not as supportive as it should have been, and the store closed on November 25, 1985. The entrance and interior of R&R are shown here on August 10, 1984. (Both, author's collection.)

Bright Pink Literature

GAY AND LESBIAN BOOKS
MUSIC • FRAMED ART • GIFTS • PRINTING
Opening by Dec. 11 • Next Door to The Body Shop
Hours: Friday. 5 pm to 2 am; Saturday and Sunday. 2 pm to Midnight • (702) 737-7780
4610 Paradise Rd., Suite 202-A • Las Vegas, NV 89109

On December 11, 1987, community advocate Rob Schlegel opened Bright Pink Literature at 4310 Paradise Road. The store's name and logo were inspired by the book *The Men with the Pink Triangle*. Schlegel stocked over 200 gay and lesbian titles and kept a bowl on the counter filled with free condoms as part of the community's fight against HIV. (Courtesy of *Bohemian Bugle*, December 1987.)

In May 1993, Wes Miller and Marlon Tinana bought Bright Pink Literature and changed the name to Get Booked. Located at Paradise Road and Naples Drive, Get Booked is still in business at the time of this writing, and has long provided the queer community with LGBTQ merchandise, information, and event space. Miller poses outside Get Booked in this photograph taken on February 14, 2002. (Author's collection.)

Dr. Charles Silverstein, author of *The Joy of Gay Sex*, is interviewed at Get Booked by journalist Jennifer Marino on April 29, 1999. (Author's collection.)

Noted female impersonator Frank Marino from Las Vegas' "An Evening at La Cage" held a book signing for his autobiography, *His Majesty, the Queen*, at Get Booked on January 19, 1997. From left to right are Wes Miller, Get Booked owner; Marino; unidentified contest winner; and community advocate Terry Wilsey. (Author's collection.)

It was the community of female impersonators, like Billy Richards, who first built a bridge between the straight and queer communities. In 1938, Richards played the Fremont Tavern and the Green Shack restaurant and nightclub in Las Vegas, where he was noted as "The Entertainment Sensation of the World!" (Author's collection.)

Las Vegas' Kit Kat Club, at the intersection of Fremont Street and Charleston Boulevard, hosted drag reviews as early as 1943. Noted as "Nevada's Gayest Night Club," the Kit Kat was declared out-of-bounds for eager soldiers stationed at the nearby Las Vegas Army Airfield. (Both, courtesy of the Clark County Museum.)

DUKE WILEY'S (Khoury's) EL RANCHO RIO

presents . . .

AMERICA'S NO. 1 FEMALE IMPERSONATOR

. . . The Second Julian Eltinge

LUCIAN
The Male Sophie Tucker

Throughout the 1940s, female impersonators performed in small clubs along the Las Vegas Strip and the Boulder Highway. This program is from a revue by famed impersonator Lucian, who appeared at the El Rancho Rio nightspot in 1949. (Courtesy of Robert "Bob" Stoldal.)

Joey Skilbred, whose stage name was Jocelyn Somers, was one of Las Vegas' most beloved impersonators. Skilbred began performing in Las Vegas in the early 1970s and eventually joined the troupes of Kenny Kerr's "Boylesque" and Frank Marino's "An Evening at La Cage." Skilbred died in 1996. (Author's collection.)

Kenny Kerr was the first female impersonator whose performances became a Las Vegas entertainment tradition. Kerr's "Boylesque" opened at the Silver Slipper Casino's Gaiety Theatre on Friday, May 13, 1977. Kerr became one of the queer community's most ardent advocates and paved the way for such later female impersonation productions as Frank Marino's "An Evening at La Cage." Kerr died on April 18, 2013. (Author's collection.)

Drag shows have long been performed in Las Vegas' queer bars and nightclubs. Among the most popular of these shows was the Gospel Brunch, featuring the Reverend Wilhemina Parsons and the Baptist Boys. Pictured here at the Spotlight Lounge on February 11, 2001, are, from left to right, the Reverend Wilhemina (Bill Schafer) and the Baptist Boys (Kevin Hall, "Mother" Brian Babcock, and Bret Franta). (Author's collection.)

The Gospel Brunch's Church Ladies are pictured at the Spotlight Lounge on February 11, 2001. From left to right are Kitty Litter (Marcus Grissom), Ivana Diamond (Rob Wright), Miss Frankie (Frank Feliz), Bella DeBall (Gary Klein), Ida Slapther (Terry Friedman), Truly LaFemme (David Miller), and Dita B (Brenton Lago). (Author's collection.)

On September 18, 1985, "An Evening at La Cage" opened at the Riviera Hotel in Las Vegas. Frank Marino became principal in the show shortly after it opened and, like Kenny Kerr before him, became one of the Las Vegas queer community's greatest boosters. This cast photograph was taken on November 29, 2002. (Courtesy of Frank Marino.)

Two

Establishing Politics

With its social identity established through such shared venues as bars, bookstores, and bathhouses, as well as by the popular vehicle of female impersonation, the Las Vegas queer community needed to develop a political consciousness. It was the American Civil Liberties Union on September 20, 1977, during a human rights seminar at the Clark County Library, that first urged the Las Vegas LGBTQ community to organize and fight for its rights. "There is a lot to be afraid of," Tom Hartman, cochairman of the Gay Rights National Lobby, warned, "but we have the power to overcome the danger if we organize."

From that challenge grew the community's first publication, the *Vegas Gay Times* (in 1978), and its first political organization, Nevadans for Human Rights (in 1979). Within a few years, NHR was joined by the Metropolitan Community Church (MCC) in 1979, the Nevada Gay Action League in 1980, and the Gay Academic Union (GAU) at the University of Nevada, Las Vegas in 1982. A decade later, the Gay and Lesbian Community Center of Southern Nevada was established; it has flourished, and today serves as the tie that binds together the Las Vegas queer community. Las Vegas' first Pride event—known then as the First Annual Human Rights Seminar—was held on the UNLV campus in 1983, while the city's first National Coming Out Day was celebrated on October 11, 1991.

Despite the support queer organization promises, lesbians and transgender people have often felt left out and have established independent communities of their own. Women have contributed in significant and fundamental ways to the larger queer community as bar owners, journalists, photographers, political advocates, and religious figures. The transgender community, while slow in organizing itself and advocating for its rights, has made rapid strides. In a political trifecta unmatched by any other state, in 2011, the Nevada Legislature passed and the governor signed three pieces of trans-inclusive legislation.

The importance of the political development of Las Vegas' queer community is best described by Anne Mulford, who had not been out of her closet very long when she attended the 1991 National Coming Out Day celebration. "I thought I was so brave," Mulford says. "I remember being up on the stage with everybody dancing towards the end of the festival. I was celebrating finally knowing who I was. Who I *am*. It was very joyful for me."

Gays may challenge LV casinos

By NED DAY
Times Staff Writer

Increased political activism by Las Vegas homosexuals raises the spectre of a confrontation involving Strip gaming establishments.

Homosexual activist leaders vowed this week that 35,000 Las Vegas gays will be leaving their closets in coming months to struggle for equal rights and political power in the community.

It was not until 1977 that LGBTQ Las Vegans began building a political community. On September 20 that year, the American Civil Liberties Union (ACLU) in Las Vegas sponsored a gay equal rights seminar at the Clark County Library on Flamingo Road, where it urged the queer community to organize and fight for its rights. This article was the community's first call to arms. (Courtesy of the *Valley Times*, September 22, 1977.)

NONE.

	Individual	Joint
Basic Membership	$20	$30
Contributing Membership	$35	$50
Supporting Membership	$75	$75
Sustaining Membership	$125	$125

☐ New Membership

PLEASE PRINT

NAME _____

ADDRESS _____

CITY _____ STATE _____ ZIP _____

TELEPHONE NUMBER (____) _____

Are you interested in helping ACLU as a volunteer? ☐ Yes

ACLU membership automatically makes you a part of both the national organization, your state affiliate and local chapters where they exist.

GAY RIGHT/ IN NEVADA ?

Human Rights Committee

ACLU of NEVADA
400 W Jackson
Las Vegas 89106

As an incentive for the queer community to organize, the ACLU distributed this brochure outlining the state of gay rights in Nevada. (Courtesy of UNLV Libraries Special Collections & Archives.)

Advocates Lamont Downs and Steve Hinkson, who began publishing the *Vegas Gay Times* in June 1978, founded the Las Vegas queer community's first political organization, Nevadans for Human Rights, which held its first meeting on January 13, 1979. Downs traveled to Reno, Nevada, for a television appearance—one of the queer community's earliest efforts at public advocacy. (Courtesy of *Vegas Gay Times*, April 1979.)

On October 30, 1982, Will Collins founded the Gay Academic Union. In 1983, the GAU cosponsored Las Vegas' first Gay Pride celebration with NHR and the Metropolitan Community Church. Pictured here are the GAU's founding members in March or April 1983. From left to right are (first row) unidentified, Will Collins, Christie Young, unidentified, and Julian Martin-Perez; (second row) Mike Loewy, Shawnn Slaughter, Dennis McBride, David Adams, and Ron Lawrence. (Author's collection.)

With political organizations established, the Las Vegas queer community needed a safe and open place to meet. The Gay and Lesbian Community Center of Southern Nevada opened at 912 East Sahara Avenue on September 7, 1993. Within a few months, the center was providing meeting space for community groups, HIV testing, and public programs. The center is shown here on May 30, 1998. (Author's collection.)

The Gay and Lesbian Community Center of Southern Nevada's first years were difficult, and it nearly shut down several times. In 1996, community advocate Dan Hinkley and others who wanted to save the center formed a group called Looking Forward to run board candidates who would professionalize the center. Looking Forward was successful in rescuing the community center. Hinkley became executive director and is shown here at the center on August 22, 1997. (Author's collection.)

Established in 1994, the Gay and Lesbian Community Center's annual Honorarium recognizes community members for their support and advocacy. The first recipients of the center's Honorarium, held on January 24, 1994, at the Metz Nightclub, are, from left to right, attorney Kevin Kelly, advocate Lisa Hernandez, center director David Green, advocate Lee Plotkin, and Dr. Lisa Bechtel, whose work in the AIDS community was tireless. (Author's collection.)

Among its community outreach efforts, the center sponsored a Las Vegas gay history exhibit and reception in observation of National Coming Out Day on October 8, 1998. Pictured are Reva Anderson (left), center executive director, and Tasha Hill, volunteer coordinator. (Author's collection.)

The center outgrew its first small building and, in 2002, moved into new digs in the Commercial Center at 953 East Sahara Avenue. Shown working to renovate the center's new home are, from left to right, Graham Miller, HIV prevention coordinator; Raul Mangubat, manager of Get Booked; Billy Lewis, volunteer/staff member; and Bob Bellis, executive director. (Author's collection.)

The Gay and Lesbian Community Center in Commercial Center is pictured above on August 2, 2002. The center held its grand opening on National Coming Out Day, October 11, 2002, with a ribbon cutting, as pictured below; from left to right are Clark County commissioner Dario Herrera; former Nevada state senator Lori Lipman Brown, who wrote the 1993 legislation repealing the state's sodomy law; and Nevada state assemblyman David Parks. (Both, author's collection.)

As the Las Vegas gay community found its political voice, the center became more important. Center executive director Candice Nichols and her board established a successful capital campaign called Opening New Doors to raise funds for a new building. On April 6, 2013, the center dedicated its new home at 401 South Maryland Parkway, named for the late Robert "Bob" Forbuss, community activist and philanthropist. (Author's collection.)

M. C. C.*

INVITES YOU TO

A WORSHIP SERVICE

FOR THE LAS VEGAS GAY COMMUNITY

AND THEIR FRIENDS

PROPOSED DATE:

AUGUST 26, 1979

CONTACT:

Rev. Frank D. Crouch, Jr.

5300 Santa Monica Blvd.
Suite 304

Los Angeles, CA 90029

*Metropolitan Community Church is an inter-denominational, non-discriminatory Christian
Church with a special outreach to the gay community.

FOR MORE INFORMATION CONTACT REV. FRANK AT THE ABOVE ADDRESS.

LOCATION OF THE WORSHIP SERVICE TO BE ANNOUNCED AT A LATER DATE

After an unsuccessful beginning in Las Vegas in 1974, the Metropolitan Community Church (MCC) reestablished itself in 1979. Throughout the 1980s, MCC served as the meeting place for numerous community organizations, sponsoring marriages, concerts, and auctions, as well as the first LGBTQ community bookstore, and was among the first in the community to provide help for people with HIV and AIDS. (Author's collection.)

Pictured here is an MCC baptism ceremony in Aztec Cove on the Colorado River south of Las Vegas on July 19, 1997. (Author's collection.)

On October 22, 2000, the Reverend Troy Perry, founder of MCC, dedicated the Las Vegas chapel. (Author's collection.)

Ron Lawrence, founder of the Community Counseling Center in Las Vegas, notes that the Catholic Church's proscription of queer expression is an "annihilation of human love." In response, Las Vegas gay Catholics founded a Dignity chapter in 1979. In this photograph, Bruce Adams (right) and an unidentified friend work the Dignity–Las Vegas booth at National Coming Out Day on October 9, 1994. (Author's collection.)

The LDS Church, which has a significant presence in Las Vegas business and politics, has long been hostile to the LGBTQ community. Gay Mormons, however, unwilling to leave their church, have established queer-friendly sects of their own. One is the Restoration Church of Jesus Christ, shown here recruiting at Gay Pride on May 8, 1999. (Author's collection.)

The Valley Outreach Synagogue, established in Las Vegas by Rabbi Richard Schachet in 1993, provided a home for gay Jews. Valley Outreach sponsored a booth at Las Vegas Pride on May 8, 1997. (Author's collection.)

Queer atheists Good Without a God were welcomed by the LGBTQ Humanist Council at Gay Pride on September 7, 2013. (Author's collection.)

The notorious Westboro Baptist Church of Topeka, Kansas, has picketed Las Vegas several times. The church's first Las Vegas rally occurred on March 10, 2001. At left, Westboro picketers confront a gay couple in front of the Liberace Museum on Tropicana Avenue. Pictured below are Westboro picketers at UNLV. (Both, author's collection.)

The Westboro demonstration at UNLV on March 10, 2001, drew crowds of passionate students in a counterdemonstration. At right, Joshua Dart invokes Matthew Shepard against Westboro. Below, university students counter hate with love. (Both, author's collection.)

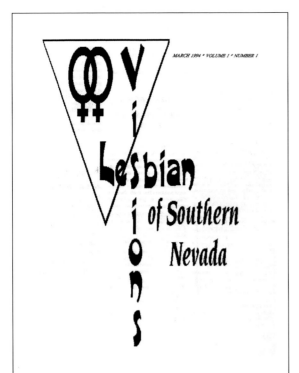

MARCH 1994 • VOLUME 1 • NUMBER 1

Lesbian Visions of Southern Nevada

Las Vegas lesbians have long complained the gay community is male-dominated, and this has often been true. While participating significantly in the broader community, lesbians have built their own independent communities. It was not until the 1990s, however, that the lesbian community found a cohesive voice through its first publication, *Lesbian Visions of Southern Nevada*, which first appeared in March 1994. (Courtesy of UNLV Libraries Special Collections & Archives.)

The Las Vegas lesbian community established its own organizations in the 1980s. One of these was Women United of Nevada (WUN), founded in 1987. WUN sponsored both social and political activities. One of its most popular social activities was its annual Valentine's Day Dance, described in this flier from 1989. WUN came to an end in 1994. (Courtesy of UNLV Libraries Special Collections & Archives.)

W.U.N. 2nd Annual

VALENTINE'S DANCE

Saturday = February 11
at the
GIPSY
4605 So. Paradise
5-9:45 P.M.

$3 MEMBER

$5 NON-MEMBER

All proceeds go to W.U.N. for future events and to the Women's Bldg. fund/
35mm photos for $2.00/Door prizes and Raffles/Memberships and Tickets for
upcoming events available/Further Information:W.U.N. Hotline: 366-8421

Established in the fall of 2000, the lesbian social group Betty's Outrageous Adventures, is still going strong in 2017. The "Bettys" are shown here on a walk along the Historic Railroad Hiking Trail near Hoover Dam on February 24, 2001. (Author's collection.)

Las Vegas' first queer theater troupe, Center Stage, Inc., was founded in 1999 by lovers and business partners Lenore Andrea Simon and Alana Brown. Over the next four years, Center Stage produced ten plays before it shut down in 2003. The production shown here is *Sappho in Love* from July 2001. (Author's collection.)

Lesbians are among the most ardent advocates for the Las Vegas queer community. One of the first such advocates was Marge Jacques, owner/manager of Le Café and Gipsy. She lectured at UNLV and provided interviews to local media. On May 7, 1983, Jacques received an award of recognition for her work during the city's first Gay Pride awards ceremony. (Courtesy of Ron Lawrence.)

In 1990, the university radio station, KUNV, began broadcasting *This Way Out*, the first internationally syndicated gay and lesbian radio program. Included in the broadcast was the *Women's Music Hour*, underwritten by Women United of Nevada, Lace women's nightclub, and Dr. Katherine Crooks. The DJ was Gerrie Blake, shown here in the studio in 1993. (Author's collection.)

One of the most popular lesbian social events in Las Vegas was the annual charity Christmas party hosted by Penny Stirling and her lover, Bree. The price of admission to the doings was one gift-wrapped toy for needy children. Stirling is shown here at her last Christmas party on December 6, 1997, before she and Bree moved to southern Utah. (Author's collection.)

Judy Corbisiero, shown here on January 18, 2008, is one of the Las Vegas community's greatest advocates. She worked tirelessly for abortion rights in Nevada, cofounded the Desert and Mountain States Lesbian and Gay Conference and the Progressive Leadership Alliance of Nevada, lobbied repeal of Nevada's sodomy law, introduced women's music to Las Vegas, and served as chairman of the Southern Nevada Stonewall Democrats. (Author's collection.)

Transgender people have been a part of Las Vegas history since before the LGBTQ community developed. Entertainer Christine Jorgensen first performed at the Sahara Hotel and Casino in 1953 and again in November 1955 at the Silver Slipper Casino. This photograph shows Christine dressed to the nines on the Silver Slipper stage, where her audience was standing room only. (Courtesy of Las Vegas News Bureau.)

Hedy Jo Star, born Carl Hammonds, was a well-known transgender entertainer and writer in the 1940s–1960s. In the 1970s, Hedy and her husband moved to Las Vegas, where she began a second career as a designer and builder of elaborate and expensive costumes for Vegas stage productions. (Author's collection.)

Yet another transgender entertainer who played Las Vegas was Jennifer Fox. Fox played the Gay 90s nightclub in North Las Vegas in 1970 and, in 1972, starred in producer Ann Corio's famous *Best of Burlesque* at Circus Circus Hotel and Casino, which ran for 22 weeks. (Both, author's collection.)

Fired from her job as an exotic dancer at Déjà vu Showgirls strip club when she outed herself in a 2003 interview with *Las Vegas City Life* magazine, Andrea Hackett became a noted transgender advocate. Hackett founded the Las Vegas Dancers Alliance and endured several confrontations with the local political establishment for her union activities and liberal politics. (Courtesy of *Las Vegas City Life*, April 14, 2003.)

In 2000, Center Stage, Inc., Las Vegas' first queer theater troupe, produced *Hidden: A Gender*, the city's first transgender play. Among those starring were former Nevada state senator Lori Brown, who wrote the legislation repealing Nevada's sodomy law in 1993, and tireless transgender advocate Jane Heenan. (Courtesy of UNLV Libraries Special Collections & Archives.)

52

The Transgender Day of Remembrance, founded in 1999 to memorialize those murdered as a result of transphobia, has been celebrated in Las Vegas since 2002. This photograph depicts the November 20, 2003, celebration, in Las Vegas. (Courtesy of Paul Ershler.)

In 2011, the Nevada State Legislature, in an extraordinary session, passed three pieces of trans-inclusive legislation. A celebration marking this victory took place on October 1, 2011, at the Progressive Leadership Alliance of Nevada offices. (Courtesy of UNLV Libraries Special Collections & Archives.)

On October 1, 2011, Equality Nevada and the Progressive Leadership Alliance of Nevada sponsored a reception celebrating passage of trans-inclusive legislation in the Nevada Legislature. In this photograph, from left to right, are Lauren Scott, transgender advocate and member of the Nevada Equal Rights Commission; state assemblyman Paul Aizley; state senator David Parks, who sponsored the legislation; and advocate Jane Heenan, expressing her appreciation. (Author's collection.)

The Gay Academic Union founded at the University of Nevada, Las Vegas in 1982, together with Nevadans for Human Rights and the Metropolitan Community Church, sponsored Las Vegas' first Gay Pride celebration in May 1983. GAU members at the Moyer Student Union include, from left to right, Christie Young, David Adams, Dennis McBride, unidentified, Rick May, unidentified, Mike Loewy, Julian Martin-Perez, Will Collins, and unidentified. (Courtesy of Ron Lawrence.)

The Moyer Student Union marquee at UNLV announcing the city's first Gay Pride celebration in 1983 was vandalized to read "Fag Pride Week." Nevertheless, the celebration, which included seminars and a Gay Pride dance, was well attended. (Author's collection.)

On May 6, 1983, Dr. Walter Herron addressed Las Vegas' first Gay Pride celebration about medical issues facing the queer community. (Courtesy of Ron Lawrence.)

Will Collins, founder of the Gay Academic Union at UNLV, was also the world's foremost Liberace impersonator. He entertained the crowd at the First Annual Gay Pride Banquet and Awards on May 7, 1983. (Courtesy of Ron Lawrence.)

Las Vegas' second Gay Pride celebration was also its first outdoor event. Pride cofounder Will Collins poses at the University of Nevada, Las Vegas events marquee on Maryland Parkway announcing the June 1984 Gay Pride. (Author's collection.)

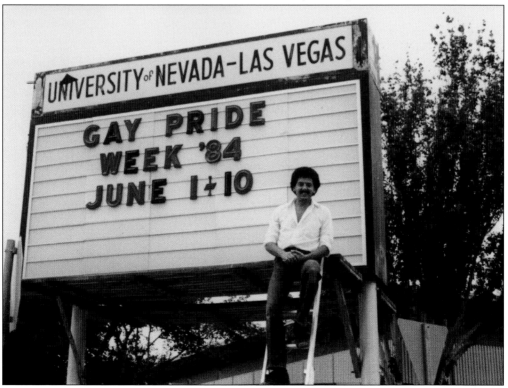

Las Vegas' 1984 Gay Pride celebration was held in Section F of Sunset Park on June 2 and featured the rock band Taa-Daa. (Both, courtesy of Christie Young.)

The First Annual Lesbian and Gay Pride Pageant was hosted at Gipsy nightclub on June 5, 1993. Successful contestants included, from left to right, Marina Kness (Ms'ter Gay Pride), Rod Tyrell (Mr. Vegas Pride), Joel Jaralillo (Miss Vegas Pride), Anne Mulford (Ms. Vegas Pride), and pageant cochairs Larry Cormier and Michael Gentille. (Courtesy of Bill Schafer.)

Las Vegas' first Gay Pride parade was held on May 10, 1997. Participants gathered behind the Flex nightclub on West Charleston Boulevard, from where they wound several miles through town to the celebration at Sunset Park. Pictured here is Marlon Tinana, owner of the Mariposa Café. (Courtesy of UNLV Libraries Special Collections & Archives.)

Las Vegas mayoral candidate Oscar Goodman, a noted attorney who defended some of Las Vegas' most notorious mob figures, embraces the gay community at Gay Pride on May 8, 1999. (Author's collection.)

Las Vegas mayor Oscar Goodman served as grand marshal for Las Vegas' first nighttime Gay Pride parade on May 11, 2001. (Author's collection.)

A reimagining of the iconic "Welcome to Fabulous Las Vegas" sign welcomed people to the Gay Pride celebration on May 12, 2002. (Author's collection.)

Three

FIGHTING FOR
LIFE AND EQUALITY

By the early 1980s, Las Vegas' queer community had finally been recognized. With its foundations set securely in political institutions like Nevadans for Human Rights, in religious organizations such as the Metropolitan Community Church, and in the dynamic social milieu of its bars, nightclubs, and Gay Pride celebration, the community was poised to begin fighting for its rights. Advocates considered how they might challenge Nevada's sodomy law and run candidates for public office to represent them. But that promise was soon swept away by the AIDS epidemic. The first AIDS death in Las Vegas was confirmed on March 10, 1983. Fighting for equal rights was postponed as the queer community not only fought against an aggressive conservative backlash grounded in AIDS hysteria, but also as it literally fought for its life. *Las Vegas Sun* columnist Muriel Stevens wrote, "Without question it is the gay community who will suffer most from the doubt and fear that is sweeping our country."

Shunned by state and local government in the worst years of the epidemic, the community had to take care of itself. Organizations such as Aid for AIDS of Nevada, the Nevada AIDS Project, Lighthouse AIDS Ministry, Golden Rainbow, and Sista to Sista were established. Heroes such as Drs. Jerry Cade, Lisa Bechtel, and Mel Pohl as well as advocates Lisa Hernandez and Wes Davis, marshaled the community. Though thousands eventually died, Las Vegas' queer community learned self-reliance and compassion and became politically savvy in fighting for care.

By the 1990s, these lessons mobilized the LGBTQ community so that it successfully fought for repeal of Nevada's sodomy law in 1993; had sexual orientation added to the list of characteristics considered to be aggravating circumstances in the crime of first-degree murder, for which enhanced sentencing could be sought in 1995; and achieved a Nevada version of the Employment Non-Discrimination Act (ENDA) in 1999. In 1996, David Parks was elected as the first openly gay state legislator in Nevada and has served ever since as the legislative voice of the state's queer community.

Three steps forward, one step back: in backlash against Nevada's ENDA, the state's conservatives—supported largely by the LDS—through initiative petition, successfully amended the state constitution to prohibit same-gender marriage. The effort opened deep and lasting social and political fissures among Nevadans. As Bob Fulkerson of the Progressive Leadership Alliance of Nevada (PLAN) said, "They're starting a war that's going to . . . be very bitter and painful. . . . This petition is not about defending marriage. It is about attacking gays and lesbians."

First case of immunity illness in LV identified

By Diane Russell
Review-Journal

The first identified case of Acquired Immune Deficiency Syndrome (AIDS) in Las Vegas has resulted in the death of a homosexual man, the Clark County chief health officer said Friday.

Speck said the man probably would not have developed pneumonia if he had not had AIDS. "If he didn't have a compromise in his immune system, he would not have become ill."

Often, the things which kill AIDS victims would not make them ill, Speck said. "In fact, these are things

AIDS had ravaged gay communities around the world for several years before the first confirmed case appeared in Las Vegas on March 10, 1983. Local columnist Muriel Stevens wrote, "Without question it is the gay community who will suffer most from the doubt and fear that is sweeping our country. . . . They worry about their jobs and about being ostracized by neighbors and co-workers." (Courtesy of the *Las Vegas Review-Journal*, March 12, 1983.)

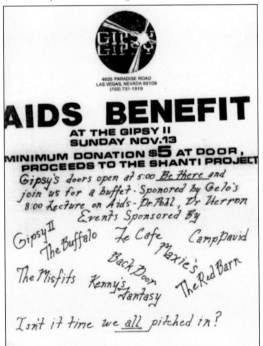

Las Vegas medical authorities were reluctant to address the AIDS epidemic, which left the queer community in the beginning to fend for itself. The first public event to address AIDS occurred on November 13, 1983, at the Gipsy nightclub. Drs. Mel Pohl and Walter Herron, both gay, addressed the illness more directly and frankly than their straight counterparts. (Courtesy of UNLV Libraries Special Collections & Archives.)

WARD - Dr. Jerry Cade says this new AIDS ward at ...rsity Medical Center will make it easier for hospital

personnel "to sit down every day, if we have to, and discus... new drugs or treatments or problems."

...DS ward to open at medical center

Because it was a public hospital whose mission was to take care of patients whatever their means, most AIDS patients in Las Vegas ended up at the University Medical Center (UMC) on Charleston Boulevard. On July 6, 1987, Drs. Jerry Cade and Mel Pohl opened the city's first dedicated AIDS ward at UMC. (Courtesy of the *Las Vegas Review-Journal*, July 6, 1987.)

Rhyolite

TOWN MEETING

Learn About the World's First
GAY COMMUNITY

Stonewall Park at Rhyolite

Located 120 Miles North of Las Vegas

You Are Invited!

Sun · Nov. 2 · 11 a.m.

BRING SACK LUNCH

Information · Express Your Opinion
Phone (702) 383-8386 or ask Operator for
Rhyolite Toll Station #2 for information.

In fighting the opprobrium aimed at the Nevada queer community during the AIDS epidemic, activists Fred Schoonmaker (left) and his lover, Alfred Parkerson (right), tried establishing a settlement where queer Nevadans could segregate in safety. One of their potential sites was Rhyolite, a ghost town outside Beatty, Nevada, where Schoonmaker and Parkerson lived in an abandoned caboose. (Above, author's collection; left, UNLV Libraries Special Collections & Archives.)

Dr. Lisa Bechtel (left), shown here with her wife, Ann Occhi, was one of the first physicians in Las Vegas to treat AIDS patients. She was honored by the ACLU as Humanitarian of the Year and by the Gay and Lesbian Community Center at its first Honorarium in 1994. Bechtel died on May 10, 1994, of AIDS, contracted from an accidental needle prick. (Author's collection.)

The famous AIDS Memorial Quilt, first produced by the NAMES Project in 1987, commemorates on quilt blocks the names of those who have died from AIDS. The Southern Nevada NAMES Project was founded in 1990. Quilt blocks are here exhibited at the Charleston Heights Arts Center, December 5, 1997, as part of the city's World AIDS Day observations. (Author's collection.)

On May 17, 1998, the University of Nevada, Las Vegas hosted the 15th annual AIDS Candlelight Vigil where the Las Vegas AIDS Memorial Garden was dedicated. (Author's collection.)

In May 1998, the Spotlight Lounge sponsored a fundraiser for Reach Out, which stands for "Relieving Each AIDS Child's Hurt, Our Ultimate Task." (Courtesy of Bill Schafer.)

Lighthouse Compassionate Care, which grew out of Rev. Sarah Serna's AIDS Pastoral Care Coalition in 1994, sought to address the spiritual needs of the AIDS community. Shown here is a Lighthouse fundraising sale of the cookbook *101 Men Who Love to Cook* on March 22, 1998. From left to right are Wes Miller, Rolando Guerrero, Richard Powell, and Rob Schlegel. (Author's collection.)

Cofounded by Reva Anderson, former executive director of the Gay and Lesbian Community Center, Sista to Sista (Sisters Informing Sisters on Topics about AIDS) was one of many organizations born out of the queer community to care for HIV-positive brothers and sisters. The Sista to Sista booth is shown here at the Gay Pride fest on May 12, 2002. (Author's collection.)

Gay activists work against sodomy law

☐ State laws and attitudes make Nevada unfriendly territory, but gay rights are emerging anew in politics.

In statute since 1861, Nevada's sodomy law, known as Nevada Revised Statute 201.190, was a handy tool for terrorizing the state's gay men. Repealing it seemed an overwhelming task, but in 1992, with the resolve and self-reliance it learned in caring for itself through the AIDS epidemic, Nevada's queer community pooled its energy and resources to lobby the state legislature to repeal 201.190. (Courtesy of the *Las Vegas Review-Journal*, June 14, 1992.)

It was freshman state senator Lori Lipman Brown, schoolteacher and attorney, who introduced Senate Bill 466 on May 13, 1993, to repeal the state's sodomy law. (Author's collection.)

68

The queer community hired a lobbyist and set up a toll-free call line to argue for repeal of Nevada's sodomy law in the state legislature. Community representatives in the state capital of Carson City convinced legislators that repealing the sodomy law was good for Nevada and its tourist-based economy. (Courtesy of UNLV Libraries Special Collections & Archives.)

CALL NOW! 1/800-367-5057
to register your support with the State Assemby for

SB466

the repeal of the 'Crimes Against Nature' law.
(commonly known as the 'sodomy law')

CALL NOW! 1/800-367-5057
to register your support with the State Assemby for

SB466

the repeal of the 'Crimes Against Nature' law.
(commonly known as the 'sodomy law')

CALL NOW! 1/800-367-5057
to register your support with the State Assemby for

SB466

the repeal of the 'Crimes Against Nature' law.
(commonly known as the 'sodomy law')

CALL NOW! 1/800-367-5057
to register your support with the State Assemby for

SB466

the repeal of the 'Crimes Against Nature' law.
(commonly known as the 'sodomy law')

8A LAS VEGAS SUN Thursday, June 17, 1993 a

LEGISLATURE '93

Miller quietly signs bill lifting gay-sex ban

By Cy Ryan
SUN CAPITAL BUREAU

CARSON CITY – With little fanfare, Gov. Bob Miller has signed a bill repealing a 1911 law that prohibits sexual acts between consenting adults of the same gender.

The law becomes effective immediately.

islation.

"We realize he had many people calling in opposition," Kelly said.

But most elected officials, he said, know there is a strong telephone network in Nevada that does not represent the average person.

This bill, he added, "provides

whether the sex show, which people paid to see, was in public.

The new law makes it a felony to have anal intercourse, cunnilingus or fellatio in public.

Miller is Catholic, and the Catholic Church does not favor homosexuality. But Kelly, also a Catholic, in urging passing of the bill presented an affidavit from

to homosexuals is not a violation of the faith.

"Even though the church does not embrace homosexuality, it doesn't suggest we discriminate," Kelly said.

The bill was one of the most controversial in the Legislature and drew opposition from

lead to schools teaching about the homosexual lifestyle.

Assemblyman John Bonaventura, D-Las Vegas, was one of

the bill's main critics.

islator sent letters to so dents, saying, "The repretives who vote for this bill be thrown out of office."

The repeal effort worked and at 6:02 p.m., June 16, 1993, Democratic governor Bob Miller signed SB 466, ending more than a century of repression against Nevada's queer community. (Courtesy of the *Las Vegas Sun*, June 17, 1993.)

Backlash against Nevada's sodomy law repeal was swift. On January 25, 1994, the Nevada Citizens Alliance (NCA) worked to put the Minority Status and Child Protection Act (MSCPA) on the Nevada ballot. The MSCPA forbade domestic partnership, spousal benefits, or "marital status" for gay Nevadans and would keep public library books about homosexuality restricted to adults. Shown here is Lon Mabon of the NCA. (Courtesy of *Advocate* magazine.)

The campaign in support of the MSCPA was ugly. The Independent American Party in Nevada, founded by the Mormon Hansen family, joined the campaign. An editorial cartoon from the *Las Vegas Review-Journal* expresses the horror many felt over the MSPCA. By the June 21, 1994, deadline for filing completed petitions, the NCA had failed to gather enough signatures and the MSCPA died. (Courtesy of the *Las Vegas Review-Journal*, Sunday, June 19, 1994.)

Perhaps more important than repealing Nevada's sodomy law was protecting queer citizens in their jobs. In 1999, gay Nevada state assemblyman David Parks introduced AB 311, Nevada's version of an Employment Non-Discrimination Act (ENDA). Parks here addresses a pro–AB 311 rally at the University of Nevada, Las Vegas, on March 21, 1999. (Author's collection.)

Showing their support for AB 311 at the university rally on March 21, 1999, are, from left to right Alexis Sáinz (field organizer, National Gay and Lesbian Task Force), Holly Carratelli (Gay and Lesbian Community Center), Reva Anderson (Gay and Lesbian Community Center), Nevada state assemblyman David Parks, former Nevada state senator Lori Lipman Brown, Susan Carratelli (Southern Nevada Association of Pride, Inc.), and Tasha Hill (Gay and Lesbian Community Center). (Author's collection.)

Nevada's ENDA legislation passed both houses of the legislature and was signed into law by Republican governor Kenny Guinn. At a victory rally at Keys nightclub on July 4, 1999, Nevada's US representative Shelley Berkeley honored state assemblyman David Parks. (Author's collection.)

It was during the 1990s that the Las Vegas queer community found its political voice. Las Vegas became a popular stopover for gay and gay-friendly politicians from across the country. A reception honoring Candace Gingrich, Newt Gingrich's lesbian half sister, served as a fundraiser for the Gay and Lesbian Community Center of Southern Nevada on December 12, 1997. Pictured from left to right are Anne Mulford, Gingrich, and Vincent Frey. (Author's collection.)

Gay Massachusetts congressman Barney Frank addresses the Las Vegas queer community at the first annual dinner of the Gay and Lesbian Democratic Caucus on June 2, 2000. (Author's collection.)

The University of Nevada, Las Vegas hosted the Millennium Youth Conference in the Moyer Student Union on July 14, 2000. Pictured are Monera Matthews (left) and Lara Moser. (Author's collection.)

On July 28, 2000, community advocates Ron Lawrence and Dan Hinkley hosted a fundraiser for Beth Wachsman, who was running for family court judge, Department K in Clark County, Nevada. From left to right are Vincent Frey, Antioco Carrillo, Lori Brown, Hinkley, Lawrence, Beth Wachsman, and her wife, Laura Granich. (Both, author's collection.)

Taking its place alongside traditional political parties, the queer community of Las Vegas founded the Southern Nevada Stonewall Democrats in July 2001. The organization's first public meeting was hosted on July 21, 2001, at the home of community advocates Ron Lawrence and Dan Hinkley. (Author's collection.)

Dan Hinkley addresses the Southern Nevada Stonewall Democrats at their first public meeting on July 21, 2001. (Author's collection.)

The fight for same-gender marriage began in Las Vegas in 1996 when Christina Sealander and Royce Kohler established the Equal Right to Marry Project and the Nevada Freedom to Marry Coalition. The project's first public event was a series of symposiums and workshops on same-gender marriage. Pictured from left to right are Royce Kohler, Mike Flower, and Antioco Carrillo at the Clark County Library on August 2, 1996. (Author's collection.)

Featured speaker at the Equal Right to Marry Project's first public seminar on August 2, 1996, was noted Lambda Legal Defense and Education Fund attorney Evan Wolfson. (Author's collection.)

On National Freedom to Marry Day, February 12, 1998, the Nevada Freedom to Marry Coalition sponsored a mass holy union ceremony on the steps of the Foley Federal Building in downtown Las Vegas. (Author's collection.)

Metropolitan Community Church Rev. David Gillentine performed a mass holy union ceremony on the steps of the Foley Federal Building in downtown Las Vegas on February 12, 1998. (Both, author's collection.)

Honoring National Freedom to Marry Day on February 12, 1998, the University of Nevada, Las Vegas hosted an ACLU "Teach-In" on same-gender marriage in the Moyer Student Union. Pictured from left to right are Metropolitan Community Church reverend David Gillentine, Katie Steinkamp, Dennis McBride (speaking), Gary Peck (ACLU of Nevada), Reva Anderson (Gay and Lesbian Community Center), and former Nevada state senator Lori Brown (author of the state's 1993 sodomy law repeal). (Author's collection.)

On April 25, 1998, Metropolitan Community Church reverend B.J. "Beau" McDaniels performed a mass holy union ceremony at the Gay Pride celebration. (Courtesy of UNLV Libraries Special Collections & Archives.)

On January 4, 2000, the Coalition for the Protection of Marriage in Nevada (CPM) filed an initiative petition to collect signatures to place on the ballot Question 2, a Nevada version of the federal Defense of Marriage Act. Pictured here are competing campaign signs: above is "Yes on 2" from the CPM, and below is "No on #2" from the gay community's Equal Rights Nevada organization. (Both, author's collection.)

Equal Rights Nevada's first press conference was hosted by Christ Episcopal Church in Las Vegas on September 11, 2000. Richard Ziser (center), director of the Coalition for the Protection of Marriage in Nevada, attended and took notes. (Author's collection.)

Despite a valiant fight, Equal Rights Nevada and the queer community were outnumbered and out-funded. On November 5, 2002, Question 2 passed, and the Nevada Constitution was amended to forbid same-gender marriage in Nevada and to forbid Nevada from recognizing same-gender marriages from others states and nations where it was legal. (Courtesy of the *Las Vegas Review-Journal*, November 6, 2002.)

QUESTION 2

Same-sex marriage ban wins for second time

Richard Schlegel, executive director of Equal Rights Nevada, is shown Tuesday outside the Gay & Lesbian Community Center.

Constitutional question required approval in two consecutive elections

Four

The Queering
of Las Vegas

Las Vegas' queer community at the time of this writing has made astounding progress. Queer Las Vegans built their community despite suppression by a homophobic legal system, the scourge of AIDS, and political and religious censure. Development of that community has been inspiring, as gay Nevadans have transformed themselves from pariahs to equal citizens. The 11 years from 2005 through 2016 worked profound changes in the state to the benefit of its queer population. In 2009, the Nevada state legislature overrode the governor's veto to pass domestic partnership legislation. While the state's constitution still prohibited same-gender marriage, domestic partnership provided nearly all the same rights, responsibilities, and benefits on the state level. As former Las Vegas mayor Jan Jones Blackhurst—long a champion of Las Vegas' LGBTQ community—wrote in support of the bill, "Our state cannot afford to lose any more revenue to other destinations because of a reputation as a place which is not socially or politically the right place to do business or to vacation." It took the US Supreme Court decision *United States v. Windsor* in 2013 in part to move the Ninth US Circuit Court of Appeals to specifically strike down Nevada's ban of same-gender marriage. In justifying that decision, Judge Stephen Reinhardt wrote that, "When same-sex couples are married, just as when opposite-sex couples are married, they serve as models of loving commitment to all."

In 2010–2011, with repeal of the homophobic "Don't Ask, Don't Tell" military policy, thousands of gay service men and women across Nevada were free to serve their country and the state without having to lie about or hide their orientation. On October 13–14, 2011, the nation's first professional organization for active-duty queer military personnel, OutServe, held its first conference at the New York New York Hotel and Casino in Las Vegas.

By 2006, Las Vegas had been named among the top 10 gay-friendly destinations in the United States and hotel-casinos along the famous Strip competed in marketing to the queer community. Party events such as Sunkissed, Closet Sundays, Splash, Heaven Saturdays, and Confidential became ubiquitous. Queer-identified Las Vegas advertising became common.

And as Las Vegas' queer community has assimilated more deeply into the mainstream, openly queer men and women have taken positions of influence and authority in its organizations and institutions, and been elected to the state legislature. By 2015, Nevada was among the most progressive states in the nation in supporting the legal equality of its queer citizens. In 2015, in support of the US Supreme Court's *Obergefell v. Hodges* decision that legalized same-gender marriage throughout the country, Justice Anthony Kennedy wrote of the queer community, "They ask for equal dignity in the eyes of the law. The Constitution grants them that right."

During Las Vegas' 2005 centennial celebration, the city awarded grants to produce Las Vegas–themed murals. The city's queer community received one such grant and its contribution to the centennial mural project was *Our Community*, painted on the side of the downtown building housing the Bastille nightclub at Third Street and East Imperial Avenue. This photograph was taken at the mural's dedication on October 7, 2005. (Author's collection.)

Those dedicating the Las Vegas gay community's centennial mural on October 7, 2005, are, from left to right, Markus Tracey, Brian "Paco" Alvarez, Terry Wilsey, Candice Nichols, Oscar Goodman, Lois Dohra, Grace Ann Morgan, and Marlene Adrian (Author's collection.)

In response to the 2008 success of California's Proposition 8 repealing the right to same-gender marriage, Denise Duarte and other Nevada queer advocates founded Stand OUT for Equality with the intent of securing domestic partnership rights in Nevada. On November 15, 2008, Stand OUT sponsored a rally on Sahara Avenue protesting California's Proposition 8, which drew nearly 1,000 people. (Courtesy of UNLV Libraries Special Collections & Archives.)

It's time to make a stand...

STAND OUT
FOR EQUALITY
RALLY

Saturday • November 15, 2008 • 2:00 pm

- **NOW** if the time for action!
- We will **NOT STOP** until we have the most basic rights of equality!
- It is **OUR TIME** to mobilize for justice!

Join us for sign making on Thursday @ 5:30 pm
Bring your flags to the rally on Saturday @ 2:00 pm

The Gay & Lesbian Center of Southern Nevada
953 East Sahara Avenue @ the Commercial Center
standoutforequality@thecenterlv.com
(702) 733-9800

the center

The November 15, 2008, Stand OUT for Equality rally at the Gay and Lesbian Community Center of Southern Nevada enjoyed the largest participation by the LGBTQ community of any such event. Pictured from left to right are Dennis McBride, Babs Daitch, and Dee Atwood. (Author's collection.)

The crowd at the Stand OUT for Equality rally in Las Vegas on November 15, 2008, stretched for more than a block along Sahara Avenue. (Courtesy of Babs Daitch.)

Comedienne Wanda Sykes, performing on the Las Vegas Strip, attended the Stand OUT for Equality rally on November 15, 2008, and used the opportunity to come out publicly. (Courtesy of Babs Daitch.)

Stand OUT for Equality launched a legislative lobbying effort in Carson City on April 21–22, 2009, known as Equality Days, to fight for passage of SB 283 granting domestic partnership benefits in the state. Advocate Anne Mulford (left) and Candice Nichols, executive director of the Gay and Lesbian Community Center of Southern Nevada (right), lobby Republican state assemblyman Ed Goedhart on April 22, 2009. (Courtesy of Paul Ershler.)

Nevada governor Jim Gibbons promised to veto SB 283 if it reached his desk. At a reception at the governor's mansion in Carson City on April 21, 2009, the governor's wife, Dawn—involved in a bitter divorce from her husband—supported passage of SB 283 and urged the legislature to override her husband's veto. Dawn here addresses the room in support of the LGBTQ community. (Courtesy of Paul Ershler.)

Domestic partnerships to be law

Override of veto 'a great day for fairness and equality'

By ED VOGEL and MOLLY BALL
LAS VEGAS REVIEW-JOURNAL

ASSEMBLY VOTE

CARSON CITY — Only a handful of spectators watched Sunday night as the Assembly voted 28-14 to override Gov. Jim Gibbons' veto of a bill that establishes a domestic partnership law in Nevada.

That vote, with the state Senate's 14-7 rejection of the veto Saturday, makes Senate Bill 283 a law that takes effect on Oct. 1.

Under the new law, same-sex and opposite-sex couples

INSIDE
► TEMPORARY BUDGET PATCH MIGHT MEAN STATE FUNDING SHORTFALL IN 2011 PAGE 1B

can go to the secretary of state's office, sign a registry, pay a fee and secure a domestic partnership contract that essentially gives them the same legal rights and responsibilities as married couples.

SLIDE SHOW www.lvrj.com/legislature_051109

Domestic partnerships, or civil unions, are not the same as same-sex marriages, which are now legal in five states. A constitutional amendment approved by Nevada voters in 2002 specifies that a marriage

can be between a man and a woman only.

Domestic partners do not need to solemnize their unions under the law but are free to choose to do so if they want. Employers are not required to offer medical and other benefits to domestic partner couples but may do so if they wish.

"I'm immensely pleased that the veto of the governor has been overridden," said

► SEE OVERRIDE PAGE 5A
Legislators have kind of gotten away from the moral arguments'

KEVIN CLIFFORD/THE ASSOCIATED PRESS
Rebecca Gasca and Lee Rowland, both of the American Civil Liberties Union of Nevada, hug after the Assembly voted Sunday night to override Gov. Jim Gibbons' veto of legislation allowing domestic partnerships between same-sex and opposite-sex couples.

The legislature passed SB 283, Governor Gibbons vetoed it, and the legislature then overrode his veto, establishing domestic partnership benefits for all Nevadans on May 31, 2009. (Courtesy of the *Las Vegas Review-Journal*, June 1, 2009.)

In 2012, the Lambda Legal Defense and Education Fund filed a lawsuit, *Sevcik et al v. Sandoval*, to overturn Nevada's Question 2, which prohibited same-gender marriage. On April 10, 2012, the Gay and Lesbian Community Center hosted a reception to honor the couples in Lambda's lawsuit. Pictured here are the namesakes of *Sevcik v. Sandoval*, Mary Baranovich (left) and Beverly Sevcik. (Author's collection.)

On June 26, 2013, the US Supreme Court in *United States v. Windsor* declared the federal Defense of Marriage Act (DOMA) unconstitutional. Pictured here is a June 27, 2013, rally at the Gay and Lesbian Community Center celebrating the court's decision. (Author's collection.)

Speaking at the center's June 27, 2013, rally was Nelson Araujo, an openly gay and successful candidate for the Nevada State Assembly. (Author's collection.)

Nevada state senator Patricia Spearman—African American, lesbian, and proudly progressive—was elected to the state legislature in 2012. Spearman also spoke at the center's June 27, 2013, rally celebrating the overturning of DOMA. (Author's collection.)

On October 7, 2014, the Ninth US Circuit Court of Appeals in *Sevcik v. Sandoval* struck down Nevada's Question 2, thereby giving LGBTQ Nevadans the legal right to civil marriage. Theo Small (left) and Antioco Carrillo (right) were the first same-gender couple in Clark County to receive a marriage license. (Author's collection.)

The Las Vegas queer community's political victories opened the way for LGBTQ candidates to run for party and state offices. The Lambda Business Association's January 9, 2013, meeting showcased some of these candidates and straight allies. Shown from left to right are state senator David Parks, state senator Patricia Spearman, state assemblywoman Heidi Swank, state assemblyman James Healey, and state assemblyman Andrew Martin. (Author's collection.)

On October 14, 2015, the Lambda Business Association hosted a debate among the three principal political parties in Clark County, each of which was represented by an openly gay officer. From left to right are Ed Williams, then chairman of the Clark County Republican Party; Brandon Ellyson, with the Libertarian Party of Clark County; and Chris Miller, chairman of the Clark County Democratic Party. (Author's collection.)

It was in the mid-2000s that Las Vegas' resort industry embraced the queer community. Hotels along the Las Vegas Strip began hosting entertainment and party events and advertising them openly in print ads and on billboards. This billboard advertises the Luxor Hotel and Casino's popular Temptation Sundays gay pool party, September 7, 2013. (Author's collection.)

The Gay and Lesbian Community Center grew into a major resource for the Las Vegas LGBTQ community sponsoring workshops, seminars, conferences, commemorative events, youth activities, uncensored sex-education classes, and panel discussions. The discussion shown here explored the LGBTQ African American history of Las Vegas on February 23, 2016, and featured, from left to right Andre Wade, center director of operations; Kamora Jones; Donya Monroe; and state senator Kelvin Atkinson. (Author's collection.)

Established in 1985 at the UNLV Special Collections Division, the Las Vegas LGBTQ Archive is today the most comprehensive queer collection in the Mountain West. In 2016, advocate and historian Dennis McBride donated more than 25 linear feet of queer history documents. The collection was accepted by Su Kim Chung, head of public services. (Both, author's collection.)

While the arc of Las Vegas' queer community has taken it from felony to freedom, the struggle is not finished. On June 12, 2016, the Gay and Lesbian Community Center hosted a vigil for victims of the Pulse nightclub massacre in Orlando, Florida. This vigil reminded that whether in Orlando, Las Vegas, or on the other side of the world, LGBTQ people everywhere stand as one. (Author's collection.)

Discover Thousands of Local History Books
Featuring Millions of Vintage Images

Arcadia Publishing, the leading local history publisher in the United States, is committed to making history accessible and meaningful through publishing books that celebrate and preserve the heritage of America's people and places.

Find more books like this at
www.arcadiapublishing.com

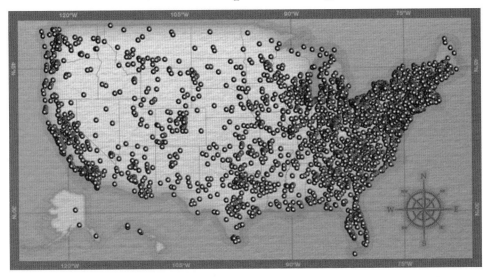

Search for your hometown history, your old stomping grounds, and even your favorite sports team.

Consistent with our mission to preserve history on a local level, this book was printed in South Carolina on American-made paper and manufactured entirely in the United States. Products carrying the accredited Forest Stewardship Council (FSC) label are printed on 100 percent FSC-certified paper.

MADE IN THE